M000283147

10 Minute Suppers for Children

ALSO BY POPPY FRASER

FANTASTIC RECIPES FROM MY
FAVOURITE PEOPLE

10 Minute Suppers for Children

Poppy Fraser

First published in Great Britain in 2015 by Fraser Publishing

DISCLAIMER: Cooking and eating involve inherent dangers. Please only undertake activities that you believe to be safe and comfortable. Fraser Publishing and Poppy Fraser assume no responsibility or liability for any damages you may experience as a result of following these recipes. All dietary indications in the recipes are a starting point for your own review, not an absolute statement of vegetarian, wheat-free, gluten-free, dairy-free or sugar-free status.

Edited, designed and produced by Tandem Publishing
http://tandempublishing.yolasite.com/

ISBN 978-0-9933811-0-2

10 9 8 7 6 5 4 3 2

A CIP catalogue record for this book is available from the British Library.

Printed and bound in Great Britain by CPI Group (UK) Ltd, Croydon CR0 4YY

This book is dedicated to my children: Lorcan, Bertie,
Constance Apple and Jacobi.

With money raised going to support Cancer Research in
memory of my own beloved father, Hugh, and for Joy,
whom I loved.

'The heart sees what is invisible to the naked eye'

CONTENTS

CANCER RESEARCH UK

A very important point about this book is that money raised from every sale will be donated to the Foreign Sisters for Cancer Research UK. Foreign Sisters UK was founded in 2007 to increase the awareness and international standing of Cancer Research UK, and to support the outstanding and vital work of its scientists and doctors. Over the past eight years, Foreign Sisters UK has raised over £600,000 for Cancer Research UK through an annual luncheon attended by women from over sixty countries based or living in London. Since 2012, the Foreign Sisters have been dedicating all of the funds they raise to The Francis Crick Institute, a new biomedical research institute in the heart of London, of which Cancer Research UK is one of the funding partners. The Francis Crick Institute will create a unique research environment equipped with cutting-edge technology.

Acknowledgements

First of all, I would like to thank Blondie, who has been the most perfect guinea pig for these recipes. He may have reduced drastically in size since I first met and cooked for him, but that bears no reflection on my recipes (ahem), it is simply indicative of his former life, which was spent in Reeves Bakery in Wilton. I am unbelievably grateful to him for his total support and love.

To my mother, whom I cannot thank enough for all her love and generosity; she is unfailingly loyal and supportive about everything I do.

We are very lucky living where we are, surrounded by the most incredible suppliers of exceptionally high-quality organic vegetables, eggs, meat and fish. It makes each step of getting food on the table a pleasure. Thanks in particular to Liz and Hugh from Kensons Organic Farm and to Jo and Phil from the Ludwell village shop.

One of the luckiest things about *10 Minute Suppers for Children* was being introduced to Sam Carter, who has helped me with all the important aspects of the book. I happened to be at Salisbury station when I met a friend on the platform who then travelled with me to London; he listened to me talking about the book and said that I needed to get in touch with Sam and very kindly set up the introduction. (Untold thanks for this, Ned.) Sam has made it possible for me to create the book as I wanted, and made it better than I could have imagined. I am so very grateful.

I want to thank Louisa Marcq for her wonderful drawings. Like Sam, I found her in the most unlikely manner. The morning after meeting Sam, when he had told me that I needed illustrations, Louisa started following me on Instagram. I loved her drawings and sent her an email asking her if she would be interested in coming up with some drawings for this book, but with the nightmarish proviso that she finished them in about three and a half days. She amazingly accepted, and I love them. Huge thanks, Louisa.

To my godchildren: Otis, Ned, Louis, Laurie, Johnny, Juno, Alice, Leila, Billy, Wren and Antonia. You give me so much pleasure, and I feel so lucky to have you in my life.

And lastly to my own children: Lorcan, Bertie, Pom Pom and Jacobi – I love you more than I could ever describe, and hope that you look back on your childhood meals as being delicious, healthy and full of love.

Preface

I started this book in 2013, when I realised I was going to have my fourth baby, eleven months after my third. I was in a panic, knowing that life was going to be rather strained, and I was working out ways to save myself from a minor breakdown. Reducing the time spent cooking was essential, freeing up precious moments to be with the children, or to lie in a darkened room, deep breathing, with a much-needed cocktail in hand.

I wrote to friends, as I had done six years before for my first book, *Fantastic Recipes from my Favourite People*, and the response was instant and wonderful. There were a few surprising replies, including poems, which transformed the book, turning it into something more special and individual. I am so grateful to all who contributed. This book is a mixture of those kind friends' recipes and my own: ones that I depend on and adore. I have included imbecilic recipes like scrambled eggs, not because you won't know how to make them, but simply as a memory jog for people whose brains are strained by children and babies. Mine is certainly scrambled to within an inch of its life.

As my fourth baby arrived we were in the middle of gutting our newly found home, so it was only in early 2015 that I felt able to sit down to finish off this now very desperately needed cookbook. I am so excited about this collection; I truly believe in each recipe, and know that every one can be cooked up in a matter of minutes, and is absolutely delicious and highly nutritious (except, perhaps, for the wildly indulgent chocolate and banana toasties).

What could be more important to our children's health than what we feed them? I believe in using as much organic, fresh, seasonal and local food as possible. Eating well to stay well is so obvious and so important.

Of course children, like us, have preferences and a right to their own personal taste, but I don't believe that we are born fussy. I do believe that if you introduce your children to a vast range of flavours and textures then they will, on the whole, be very good eaters. This book is not for fussy eaters; it is for parents who love food, believe in its importance and believe in eating what is right for us and good for our bodies and souls. It celebrates food in all its natural glory. Unprocessed, untampered with, rich in vitamins and goodness, which is what our bodies – and our children's bodies – need. It is for suppers with our children, for us to enjoy together. I eat when we are all back from school, so anytime from 5pm (frankly, the earlier the better as far as I am concerned).

Although we do eat very well at home, there are

times when my elder boys come back with blue tongues, having drunk something horrifying that they have found at the petrol station and persuaded someone to buy them. I shriek in horror, much to their delight. But I think that if we can just give them a delicious little 10-minute supper it goes a long way to counterbalance their waverings into the realms of junk, inevitable whether we like it or not. Even the most controlling mother in the world will not be able to stop her children eating something she doesn't approve of once they are released into the school system and therefore out of her clutches. It is all a question of balance in life. I think the big thing is to relax. I will never forget watching a mother dive-bomb into a bowl of hula hoops, so worried that her children were about to eat them. This was at a birthday party. I couldn't believe my eyes. I think that creating a world of contraband and restrictions results in a lot of unnecessary stress. By cooking delicious recipes, such as the ones in this book, your children are going to grow up attracted to the same wonderful, nutritious ingredients that they've already found at home.

I so hope you love this book, that your children love this book, and that you find it useful when you get back from the school run and stare blankly into the fridge, knowing that meltdowns are about to ensue unless something is put on the table pronto. The moment that the thought 'What's for supper?' comes into my head is the very moment that the stress starts to build – unless of course I have been organised and worked it all out. That is when this book, I trust, will be of great use and support. Ten minutes is not long, and it's so encouraging to see what can actually be achieved within that timeframe. Not something that's just cobbled together, but seriously delicious food we can all adore. I hope this book helps to instill a vital love of good food in your children.

Good food means good health, and nothing is more important than that.

Love, Poppy
Summer 2015

Introduction to the Author
by Sophie Edelstein

Poppy is wonderful. She is a marvellous cook, the best mother, brilliant company and everything else. Poppy, beyond anything, is also the most hilarious person I know.

Poppy also isn't strong on time, *except* in the kitchen where I feel every single time-management skill has been finely honed. Once, finally trying to leave a weekend at Poppy's (I had arrived for one night and stayed for three), I missed about five trains and got utterly held up on a country lane, all because Poppy and I decided to stop for a quick cappuccino (nothing is quick in the country, except Poppy's cooking) and sell a biscuit cake (probably the most delicious thing you'll ever eat if you can ingest that much sugar in one sitting and don't immediately contract diabetes). The biscuit cake, might I add, is Poppy's own recipe, and one that is all about timing and layering and deliciousness in the way the Romans experienced it.

While selling – and then sampling – the biscuit cake, another few trains came and went, and various meetings were missed. Poppy and I had been enjoying the time so much (this is what happens when Poppy feeds you, you get so caught up in the eating and chatting nothing else seems important) we bought back the entire thing in slices – each costing as much as we'd sold the whole thing for in the first place.

That just about sums it up. You plan to have a light snack and you stay for five meals. You miss trains, because only one thing is important – eating more with Poppy.

Poppy isn't afraid to cook healthily and every time I see her she has a newly discovered bespoke condiment (exotic nut butters anyone?) and yet, she's *real*. She can combine health with a rolled-up cigarette and a glass of wine, and this for me is the best way to prepare food, because it is done lovingly, and all so relaxed. I know my cooking is better if I've had a Scotch. I won't get distracted on that point.

At the end of the day there are so many cooking books and so many cooks, but this one is real. It is fun. You'll probably find it quite random. However, what I do know is that it is *quick*. And God knows we all need more time chatting and missing trains, so isn't that a blessing? As fun as 'slow cooking' sounds, it is much more fun to fast cook, put your children to bed and have a night on the tiles.

Store Cupboard Essentials

It is all about the quality of your ingredients – the simplest recipe is *made* by the ingredients. I would always rather eat less, but of better quality. It really matters what you buy and whom you are supporting (I really try hard to avoid buying products that use palm oil). I think the search for the cheapest weekly trolley-load is the wrong approach – it's about having a budget, and changing our diet to include delicious food that fits within that.

The following is a list of things that will help you enormously if you have them at home, squished into a cupboard or larder. The bare essentials. The list begins with oatcakes, I love them; my husband is rather fed up with them as I get them out so often, but they are seriously useful little things that remind me of home.

- Oatcakes – I like all varieties but Nairn's (thin ones) and the Stockan's triangle ones are my favourites. I use them to replace bread.
- Organic oats
- Quinoa – the red and white Merchant Gourmet pouches are insanely useful and delicious.
- Rice – I use a lot of brown rice and wild rice.
- Almonds – I do make a lot of almond milk for breakfast smoothies. That may sound virtuous and ghastly, but a milkshake is one of my favourite drinks and a dairy one brings me out in an annoying rash so that is why I stick to

the almond milk. It guarantees that you start the day with a trashed kitchen, but it's worth it.

- Hazelnuts
- Pine nuts
- Dates
- Agave nectar
- Rice noodles
- Good quality pasta
- Stock – I buy Gallo.
- Miso paste
- Flour – I have about a million different flours at home but always have some of your favourites on hand.

Tins
- Some good quality Italian tinned tomatoes.
- Coconut milk
- Chickpeas
- Butter beans

Jars
- Artichokes
- Sun-dried tomatoes
- Capers
- Cornichons
- Anchovies
- Tuna – I love the Ortiz brand or Albacore from Waitrose.
- Mustard – Dijon and grainy are the ones I use.
- Extra virgin olive oil
- Coconut oil
- Vinegar – white, red, sherry, balsamic
- Jams – I buy St Dalfour which has no added sugar.
- Organic honey

Dairy (I try to buy organic wherever it is possible, but when it comes to dairy items I think this is especially important.)
• Yoghurt – I buy goats' and sheep's yoghurt which is so delicious.
• Cheddar
• Feta
• Butter
• Eggs

Basket
• Carrots
• Onions
• Garlic
• Ginger
• Lemons
• Chillies

Herbs
• Most of them, all of the time: parsley, mint, basil, chives, coriander.

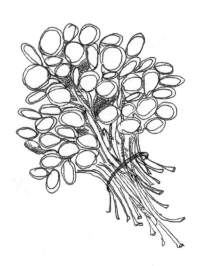

Reminders

Salt – this causes most mothers to have seizures. In fact, a doctor friend of mine from London told me that two of his patients had rushed their son into his surgery, demanding a blood test for the child, and all because they had just found out that someone had been cooking with, unbeknownst to them, salt in his food. *Please*. A little good quality sea salt in their diet is absolutely fine for children, it really is. Do season your food separately if you want; I don't. Relax and cook for them as you would for yourself.

Never use 'reduced-fat' anything in these recipes (anything 'reduced-fat' means that the food has been tampered with). These recipes are meant to be a celebration of natural products. That goes for anything 'diet' too: don't buy them, as it only means sugar has been replaced with something infinitely worse, most likely highly toxic aspartame.

The following are all ten-minute recipes, designed to help you spend just ten minutes or less in the kitchen, in and out again. Phew. The recipes do not include the use of a microwave; I have never owned one.

All recipes are for four people, two grown-ups and two children, unless otherwise stated.

At the bottom of recipes there are these initials: V, DF, SF, GF, WF – they are, I hope, helpful for people who want to avoid certain food types.

V – vegetarian
DF – dairy-free
SF – sugar-free
GF – gluten-free
WF – wheat-free

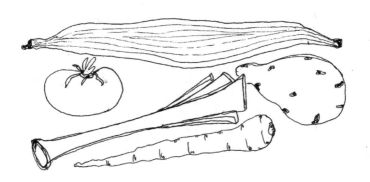

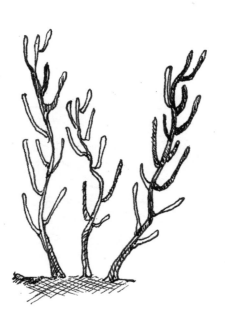

I

Soups & Salads

*L*et's start with some very quick little soup recipes, so comforting in the winter when it's dark so early. Then, as the light increases, moving onto salads, celebrating what is available to harvest. Having said that, two of these soups are raw soups and so wonderfully refreshing in the summer. I always feel incredibly happy eating raw vegetables, knowing that you are getting every possible vitamin, none being lost in the cooking process.

HACIENDA DE SAN RAFAEL GAZPACHO

The first recipe in the book has the accolade of being one of the best things I have ever tried. Saying I was about to die of excitement drinking this is true. If we can create what they create at the Hacienda then I can assure you that it is the best gazpacho you will ever taste. Now, they were unspecific with their quantities so just whizz the tomatoes and add a good glug of olive oil, and a couple of tablespoons of vinegar and adjust according to taste.

2kg of ripe tomatoes (important to buy the most amazing tomatoes you can find, full of flavour)
Extra virgin olive oil
Jerez vinegar
Salt, to taste
A little onion, peeled
1 clove of garlic, peeled

Liquidise everything, add more oil as necessary and then pass through a fine sieve for extra smoothness.

V DF SF GF WF
Full of vitamin E thanks to the tomatoes.

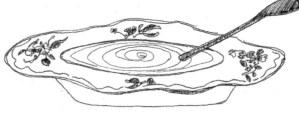

2

Raw Pea and Mint Soup

A wonderful soup that requires no cooking at all … bliss.

450g peas
800ml stock (veg or chicken)
Mint
Crème fraiche / cream

Pour a bag of frozen peas into a blender. Add fresh stock or boiling water straight from the kettle; if you are out of stock, add a tablespoon of bouillon or a vegetable stock cube and a handful of fresh mint and seasoning. Blend until smooth. Please be careful with the lid of the blender here, and don't get scorched by steam leaking out of the lid or by the boiling liquid spilling over the top of the blender. I use a tea towel to hold the lid down and open it tentatively.

Pour into bowls with a swirl of crème fraiche / cream.

V SF GF WF
Full of vitamin C thanks to the peas.

CHICKPEA SOUP

A delightfully simple, refreshing and pure tasting soup. Joyfully quick.

2 cans of chickpeas
2 cloves of garlic
6 tablespoons of olive oil
2 tablespoons of lemon juice
900ml of stock or 2 vegetable stock cubes with 900ml of hot water (I use Gallo)
A handful of mint
A handful of parsley

Strain the chickpeas and put them in a blender with the garlic, olive oil and lemon juice. Add 900ml of stock to the blender, whizz for a couple of minutes and then heat thoroughly and add some seasoning. Add the finely chopped herbs and a squeeze of lemon juice once you have ladled the soup into bowls.

V DF SF GF WF
Full of phosphorus, selenium and potassium thanks to the chickpeas, calcium and iron from the parsley.

FISH AND HERB SOUP

Fillet of white fish, skinned and cut into little chunks.
1 teaspoon coconut oil
200ml coconut milk
Handful of coriander and basil, chopped

Sauce
1 lemongrass stick
1 clove of garlic
1 shallot
1 teaspoon of lime juice
1 teaspoon of grated ginger
1 teaspoon of turmeric powder
2 teaspoons of tamari sauce

Whizz up the sauce ingredients in a blender. Heat the coconut oil in a pan and add the sauce mix, stirring away. Add the coconut milk and simmer for 8 minutes. Add the fish and put the lid on for a couple of minutes. Place everything in a bowl and scatter the herbs on top. We adore this easy fish soup.

DF SF GF WF
Turmeric is one of the best things to include in your diet: it is anti-inflammatory, rich in antioxidants and a general joy.

Mia's Leek, Pea and Potato soup

25g butter
4 leeks
250ml stock, chicken or veg
4 potatoes
Bowl of peas

Warm the butter in a pan and add the chopped leeks (white part only). Pour over the unsalted chicken or vegetable stock. Add potatoes, chopped and peeled into small pieces. Bring to boil and simmer until potatoes are soft. Add a bowl full of frozen peas and simmer until peas are ready. Blend in a mixer.

V* SF GF WF
Full of vitamin A thanks to the leeks, vitamin C from the peas and potatoes.
* If vegetable stock is used.

BROCCOLI AND HAZELNUT SALAD

I ate this salad for the first time about fifteen years ago, whilst staying with a wild, colourful Irish / Kenyan friend called Vinnie. It was on a giant beautiful platter, and has stayed in my mind ever since. As a side dish or singing on its own merits, with perhaps some rice or sourdough, it would cover all the important nutritional bases. I adore any nuts that have been roasted, and these hazelnuts are so sweet and delicious.

2 broccoli stems
1 packet of good feta
3 handfuls of cherry tomatoes
200g of hazelnuts

For the dressing
5 tablespoons of rapeseed oil
2 tablespoons of white wine vinegar
A good scrunch of black pepper
A good pinch of salt
A teaspoon of Dijon mustard

Turn your oven on to 180°C and roast the little hazelnuts for about 6 minutes. Steam the broccoli florets, cut from their stems, and place on a large plate. Chop the tomatoes into halves or quarters and scatter over the broccoli. Crumble the feta over the broccoli and tomatoes. Remove the hazelnuts from the oven and place in a tea towel. Rub the nuts within the tea towel to loosen and remove the skins, and then scatter over the broccoli salad. Combine all of the dressing ingredients and whisk and then drizzle over the salad and turn well before eating.

V SF GF WF
Full of vitamin C thanks to the broccoli, vitamin A thanks to the tomatoes. Full of magnesium, iron and vitamin B6 thanks to those hazelnuts.

CHRISTABEL'S QUINOA SALAD

Quinoa
Carrots
Cucumber
Tomatoes
Red peppers
Tamari sauce
Olive oil

Boil some quinoa for 10 minutes, then drain and rinse under cold water to cool.

Add chopped carrots, cucumber, tomatoes, red peppers, a little tamari sauce and olive oil.

A delicious healthy and quick quinoa salad!

V DF SF GF WF
A complete protein source thanks to the quinoa, which is high in vitamin E and antioxidants, and is anti-inflammatory. Can't really ask for more. Full of vitamin A thanks to the carrots, vitamin E from the tomatoes and red peppers.

Recipe for a Happy Child,
by Marina Cowdray

When Marina sent this recipe to me, it suddenly shifted the whole dynamic of the book, changing it into something more than just a collection of recipes. It gave it another dimension, and I am so grateful.

Ingredients

Love and more love.

Give your child a torch to hold, to lighten up the path of the walk called life.

Love and hug your child often and feel in your heart a connection with your child's heart. Unconditional love will flourish.

Be the change you want to see in your child. Don't turn the child into you.

Trust your intuition: feelings are more powerful than responding to your mind.

There is no such thing as routine in nature. Nature expresses itself in every given moment, let the child be a natural expression of themselves.

Take responsibility wholeheartedly for yourself, and spend time in silence. Giving yourself peace of mind that in turn gives your child peace of mind.

See yourself as the child, and remember you were the child once. Play with the child and don't take on the burdens of the world. Your child is your world.

Resistance develops from being controlled. Parents are their own conditioning: your child will repeat patterns until you understand your true nature.

When you make a mistake, be able to look your child in the eye and say sorry, please forgive me.

Drop putting yourself in the parenting role, be patient and listen fully; there is no past, there is no future, there is only this moment.

Your child is not an expression of you, they are an expression of themselves.

Transparency breeds transparency, open conversations lead to open conversations. Indoctrination of any kind is a limitation, allow your child to find their own way.

Telephoning a child constantly doesn't make a good parent. Let the child go and let the child do the calling.

Substances fill a void; when there is no void, no substances are required. Any of your own addictions will be adopted by your child, so think carefully whether you want them to repeat your patterns.

If your child upsets you, recognise your own shortcomings. Love the differences between you and your child. Look at every challenge as a blessing.

Respect and trust in your child breeds success and trust in the world.

Encouragement breeds confidence.

Drop the false belief that fitting in and being top of the class and winning a game are the priorities; this moment is the priority and let that be good enough.

Home is a place of refuge; let the child have the space they need to be quiet.

Make homework fun, otherwise don't do it.

Have deep gratitude for your child and forgive them as they are trapped in your own conditioning.

Being the perfect parent is being who you truly are. Your child is your teacher, be open to learn from your child.

Your child will bring you more joy and love than you ever imagined.

Best Pea Salad

Although this couldn't really be a meal in itself, it is possible to have this for tea with some bread and cheese, and feel that you are giving the children a vegetarian feast.

Rocket
Peas
Tin of chickpeas

Dressing
1 clove of garlic, crushed
Handful of coriander
Handful of mint
A grated knob of ginger
4 tablespoons of olive oil
Seasoning

Boil the peas and add the dressing when hot, stirring in a handful of rocket and a tinful of drained chickpeas.

V DF SF GF WF
Full of vitamins A and C thanks to the rocket, C from the peas. High levels of vitamin B6 and C from the garlic.

CLARE'S QUINOA SALAD

This is one of my favourite salads, endlessly flexible and perfect. Incredibly lazy buying vacuum packets of quinoa, but who cares – I adore them. I buy Merchant Gourmet and have them constantly in our larder as back-up. As a result this salad takes about three minutes to put together and is a complete, balanced supper.

2 packets of Merchant Gourmet Red and White Quinoa
1 small jar of chargrilled artichokes
1 small jar of sun-dried tomatoes
1 pomegranate (seeds)
2 avocados
Buffalo mozzarella or feta cheese
Salad leaves (any old mix)

Combine all the ingredients in a bowl and use some of the oil from the artichokes and tomatoes as a dressing.

V SF GF WF
A complete protein source thanks to the quinoa, which is high in vitamin E and antioxidants, and is anti-inflammatory. Full of phytonutrients, the artichokes are good for the immune system. Avocados are packed full of nutrients and goodness.

TUNA, BUTTER BEAN AND SAMPHIRE SALAD

I remember when this salad was first made, on a hot, blissful summer's day when I was panicking about what to have for lunch. This takes seconds to assemble and looks beautiful with the bright green samphire, the herbs against the tomatoes and the pale tuna.

1 jar of delicious top-quality tuna
A handful of samphire (steamed)
2 tins of butter beans
1 avocado, sliced
1 big handful of sun-dried tomatoes
A bunch each of torn-up basil and chopped parsley
A bunch of chopped spring onions

Drain the butter beans, place them and all of the other ingredients in a lovely bowl. Scatter the herbs on top and toss thoroughly.

DF SF GF WF
Full of vitamins A, B and C thanks to the samphire.

'But life is what you make of it, and when you have the confidence to go out and follow your dreams it can take you on an incredible journey.'

Gerald Ogilvie Laing

II

Fish

*F*ish is an ideal ingredient for many 10-minute suppers; it is of course so good for us and for the development of growing brains. I do hope it somehow stops mine from shrinking. Be careful not to overdo it though: a great friend was given so much fish as a child (her mother fully subscribing to the brain theory) that she hasn't touched it since. She and her siblings are all Oxbridge scholars, however, so her mother may feel she's proved her point.

Growing up we used to have a fishman, Eddie the Fish, who would come once a week to our door in the Highlands – it was always so exciting rushing out to the van to see what that day's catch was. He would open up the back doors and his bright blue eyes would sparkle as my mother would ask, 'Anything exciting this week, Eddie? Lobbie? Crab?' More often than not he would have wonderful monkfish or lemon sole.

I think of fish now as such a treat in an uncertain world, where fish are being caught in such irresponsible ways, devastating our stocks.

Please look for the MSC label on packets of fish if you are buying in a supermarket; this way you are rewarding fisheries that are committed to sustainable fishing practices. Otherwise, please only support fishmongers who source fish responsibly.

THE MOST DELICIOUS TUNA STEAKS

These steaks are possibly my favourite recipe in the whole book, inspired by Delia Smith's dish. It is often quite difficult to find really good pink tuna steaks, but when I do, my mouth waters at the thought of this recipe. My boys adore grainy mustard and the zing from the lime juice here.

Tuna steaks, 1 per person
2 tablespoons of capers
2 tablespoons of white wine vinegar
4 tablespoons of olive oil
A big bunch of chopped coriander
1 tablespoon of wholegrain mustard
1 garlic clove, pressed
1 shallot, finely chopped
Juice and zest of a lime

Griddle your steak, and warm all of the ingredients for the sauce. Pour over the steak and serve.

We eat these with boiled new potatoes and peas.

DF SF GF WF

GOUJONS

I think these are quicker to make than fish fingers baked in the oven, and a lot tastier.

2 fillets of white fish
3 slices of bread
1 egg
Butter and oil for frying

Get your fishmonger to fillet and take the skin off the white flesh. I often use monk for goujons, or cod, haddock or plaice. Anything will do really.

Whizz up a couple of slices of bread in the magimix; I only blend for a few seconds as I prefer the breadcrumbs to be large and not blended to a fine flour.

Heat up a tablespoon of butter (with a dash of olive oil in the pan to stop the butter from burning). Whisk up an egg, and dip little bits of the fish in the egg, followed by the breadcrumbs. Fry them gently in the pan once the butter is foaming, on a medium heat. Give them a couple of minutes on each side and then serve with peas and steamed spinach, new potatoes or rice.

As an alternative to this you can use lemon sole fillets, one per person, which I leave whole. Both are mouth-watering, light and delicious.

Steamed Hake

One of my very favourite memories of fish – this steamed hake recipe my mother made for me once. She used a bamboo steamer and we ate it with new potatoes covered in butter and mint. You can of course substitute any white fillets for the hake.

Hake, enough for you all
A generous handful of chives, mint, parsley and basil
Extra virgin olive oil

Simply place the skinned, filleted hake in your steamer with the chopped herbs and a drizzle of the olive oil. Steam for about 4 minutes, or until you think it is ready – it will not take long.

Remove and season. As simple as it gets, and equally as delicious.

DF SF GF WF

Wild Salmon and Noodles in Miso Broth

I think is important to know that the days of eating cheap salmon as a staple food are numbered. If we want to eat sustainable fish then we must change our habits. Please avoid buying farmed salmon (organic salmon is not much better) on health grounds. The fish is full of toxic chemicals like PCB and added colourants. Buy wild salmon as a precious treat or more abundant fish like mackerel.

Salmon fillets
Rice noodles
Coriander
Miso paste
1 carrot (peeled with a peeler into long strips)
1 mild red chilli
1 clove of garlic, grated or very finely sliced
A knob of ginger, sliced very finely
Spring onions

This salmon in miso broth is smoky and fulfilling. Start by making the miso broth: either use a sachet of miso soup or paste, adding hot water. Toss the garlic, chopped spring onions, carrots, chilli and ginger into the broth and heat until simmering. Add the noodles and salmon on top, place the lid on, and cook on a low heat for 4 minutes. Serve in a bowl with the chopped coriander sprinkled on top.

DF SF GF WF

THE STOURTONS' GLUTEN-FREE
SALMON FISHCAKES

This is a fantastic recipe which has one slight cheat: you have to have cold mash in the fridge. I've included it though as a 10-minute recipe because it's too good not to.

1 adult portion of cold mashed potato from fridge
2 salmon fillets (please read my thoughts about farmed salmon on previous page)
A handful of parsley / chives
A squeeze of lemon juice
French mustard (optional)
Black pepper (optional)

'These quantities produce fishcakes that are jam-packed with salmon. If you wanted to stretch the recipe just add more mashed potato. This is a winning supper for our three girls.

'It is important the mashed potato is from the fridge, as ideally you would want these fishcakes prepared in advance and to sit in the cold, as this makes them 'set' and prevents them falling apart. The cold mashed potato skips out this stage, making it super speedy. Another missed stage is that I do not breadcrumb them. This saves on washing-up and time. You therefore fry the potato and salmon directly to crisp them up – more delicious than crispy breadcrumbs.

'Cook the salmon on a greased baking tray for 4–5 minutes in a hot oven. It does not matter if they are not completely cooked through. Take the cooked salmon off the skin and put it in a bowl with the cold mashed potato. Add the chopped chives / parsley and a squeeze of lemon juice. If your children like stronger tastes add the black pepper and mustard. With a fork flake up the salmon and mix with all the ingredients. Using your hands, form the mixture into fishcakes, whichever size suits.

'Fry for about 2–3 minutes on each side until crispy and warmed through.'

DF SF GF WF
Full of omega 3 fatty acids, thanks to the salmon.

Rosie's Cod with Pesto and Parma Ham

Pre-heat the oven to 180°C. Put a layer of pesto on top of cod fillets and wrap each one in Parma ham. Put in a baking tray with baby tomatoes on the vine. Roast in the oven for 10 minutes and serve with steamed baby potatoes and greens.

DF SF GF WF
Full of vitamin B12, iodine and selenium thanks to the cod.

SARDINES WITH VINE TOMATO AND
RED ONION SALSA

6 medium sardines, washed, gutted and filleted by your fishmonger
500g plum vine tomatoes
2 limes
Half a red chilli (seeds removed)
1 small red onion
1 small bunch of fresh coriander
Thyme

Heat the oven to 180°C. Check the sardines for bones and drizzle a little olive oil over a baking tray and sprinkle with thyme. Lay the fillets on top, skin side up and sprinkle with more thyme and salt and olive oil. Place in the oven for 8–10 minutes until the skins crisp up.

Meanwhile soak the tomatoes in boiling water for 15 seconds, then plunge into cold water and remove their skins. Cut into halves and take out the seeds with a teaspoon, then dice the flesh. Add the juice of the limes, the chopped-up chilli and diced onion. Mix and add the coriander. Serve beside the sardines on each plate.

DF SF GF WF
Full of vitamin B12, selenium and omega 3 thanks to the sardines, and vitamin A and E from the tomatoes.

TUNA BALLS

200g tuna in olive oil
115g breadcrumbs (gluten-free if preferred)
85g ricotta
Zest of 1 lemon
Bunch of basil, chopped
1 egg
Black pepper

Tip the tuna, drained from the oil, into a bowl. Add the breadcrumbs, ricotta, lemon zest, basil and egg. Mash all together and add the pepper. Using floured hands, make little balls out of the mixture. Fry in a little heated olive oil for about 6 minutes until golden.

We eat these with this tartare sauce, which is so quick and easy.

Tartare Sauce
Take 3 tablespoons of mayonnaise.
Add the juice of half a lemon.
Chop up a handful of gherkins very small.
Add 2 tablespoons of tiny capers, roughly chopped.
1 tablespoon of white wine vinegar.
1 tablespoon of chopped parsley.

Combine all these in a bowl and serve with the balls.

GF* WF*
Full of vitamin A and B12 thanks to the tuna.
* Provided gluten-free crumbs are used

SALMON STIR-FRY

Salmon fillets, 1 per person (please see my feelings about salmon on page 22)
Either a bag of chopped-up stir-fry vegetables, or chop yourself a handful of cabbage, of all different varieties. Add a couple of carrots, peeled and sliced, and a handful of spinach.
Sesame oil
2 cloves of garlic, finely sliced
A knob of ginger, finely sliced
A lemon or lime
Tamari sauce

Heat up some sesame oil in a pan and very gently fry the garlic and ginger for a couple of minutes without browning the garlic. Add the salmon fillets (skins removed) and cook for a further couple of minutes and then add the chopped vegetables and stir for a further couple of minutes. Whilst cooking, sprinkle some tamari sauce over the stir-fry, and a squeeze of lemon or lime. Take it off the heat as soon as the vegetables look gently cooked.

DF SF GF WF
Full of omega 3 fatty acids thanks to the salmon. Full of vitamins C and K and iron thanks to the cabbage and spinach.

MOULES MARINIÈRE
(ALWAYS THINKING OF NEL AND MATT)

What a wonderful way of introducing romance to children through their supper. I don't know why I think of moules as being so romantic ... but I do. I remember turning up for supper on the wrong night once at Nel and Matt's house in Dorset. I wondered why it seemed so quiet as I knocked on the door. I went round and knocked on the kitchen window as the door was unanswered, and there were my hosts sitting together, having a lovely bowl of moules with crusty bread. A dreamy night.

Such fun for children to pull out the moules, and eat with a chunk of wonderful bread dunked into the sauce.

1kg mussels
2 shallots, finely chopped
2 sprigs of thyme, leaves picked
1 bay leaf
150ml dry white wine
50g butter, cubed
A small bunch of flat-leaf parsley, finely chopped

Rinse the mussels in cold running water, and then give them a good scrub and scrape to remove any barnacles and dirt. Discard any with broken shells, and give any open ones a sharp tap: if they don't close, then throw them away too, because they're dead. Pull out the beards – the fibrous little appendages which the mussels use to attach themselves to ropes or rocks.

Put the chopped shallots, thyme leaves, bay leaf and wine into a large pan, and bring to a simmer. Turn the heat down, and cook gently for 7 minutes, then turn up the heat to medium-high. Drain the mussels and tip into the pan. Cover and cook until most of them have opened: about 3 minutes.

Add the butter and put the lid back on for 30 seconds to allow it to melt. Add the parsley and shake the pan well to distribute, then season gently and serve immediately, discarding any mussels that remain closed.

SF GF WF
Full of iron and vitamin B12 thanks to the moules.

A Sardine Parcel

This method can be applied to any fish, as they all taste wonderful cooked in this way. I love bringing the parcel to the table, piercing a hole in the foil and watching a fragrant waft of steam emerge, before I tear the foil open, revealing perfectly cooked fish.

Sardines
A clove of garlic, sliced
A knob of ginger, peeled
Whatever herbs you have available. I use flat-leaf parsley, basil, chives or coriander.
Extra virgin olive oil

Lay some sardines or mackerel fillets, or loins of other fish, on a large piece of foil. Decorate the fish with slices of ginger, a few slices of garlic, some fresh herbs (parsley, basil, chives or coriander). Drizzle in good extra virgin olive oil and season. Fold the foil over to form a parcel and seal the edges by folding over a few times to create a sealed envelope.

Pop in a hot oven, 180 / 200°C, for 8 minutes. We eat this with a green salad.

DF SF GF WF
Full of vitamin B12, selenium and omega 3 thanks to the sardines.

ROASTED COD AND TOMATOES

I remember posting an image of this supper on Instagram and getting sweet responses as Jacobi's podgy hand was in shot, reaching for the tomatoes. We all love this incredibly simple supper.

Cod fillets
Chopped ripe, wonderful tomatoes
1 finely sliced garlic clove
Handful of basil
Half a red chilli
Extra virgin olive oil

Heat up your oven to 180°C. Meanwhile, place the fish pieces in a baking tray and scatter the tomatoes, garlic and basil and chilli on top. Drizzle with extra virgin olive oil and bake for 10 minutes. Perfect!

DF SF GF WF
Full of vitamin D, phosphorus and selenium thanks to the cod. Vitamin E and A from the tomatoes.

ALEX'S TUNA BOLOGNESE

'So basic, but Tilly and Teddy LOVE my tuna Bolognese. Always a failsafe when the fridge is empty.'

Chop an onion very fine and soften in the pan with a glug of rapeseed oil. Boil some water and cook gluten-free spaghetti. Add a can of tinned tomatoes to the onions and cook for 10 minutes. Then stir in a can of tuna (soaked in olive oil). A teaspoonful of honey is optional.

Serve with some finely grated Parmesan.

Full of vitamin A and B12 thanks to the tuna.

LITTLE MAGIC GEMS

These are fun to eat for children, building their own parcel from the little gems. A messy, quick, delicious supper.

Little gem lettuce, one or two per person
Prawns or chicken (or any leftover meat you may have)
Cucumber
Avocado
Coriander
Lime

You can add any fish or meat that you may have left over in your fridge. If you don't, gently fry some prawns in a pan, or some chicken fillets cut into strips for a few minutes until ready.

Break up the gems into their individual leaves and load up with chopped-up cucumber sticks, chopped-up coriander, slices of avocado and topped with a squeeze of lime.

DF SF GF WF
Full of vitamin K thanks to the cucumber, vitamin C from the avocado.

Emily's Smoked Haddock Croquettes

Emily runs the award-winning Kingham Plough in Oxfordshire and is well known as an incredible chef. For those like me, unfamiliar with the term 'pane', it means coating in breadcrumbs and frying.

500g natural smoked haddock (skinned and filleted)
1 large potato
Bay leaf
Parsley
4 peppercorns
Lemon
Chives

For the sauce
50g plain flour
50g butter
300ml milk, infused with the smoked haddock
1 egg

To *pane*
Eggs
Flour
Breadcrumbs

Weigh out the fish and cut it into equal-sized cubes. Peel and dice the potato.

Bring the milk to the boil with the parsley stalks, pepper, bay leaf and half a lemon. Add the fish and potato and reduce to a simmer. When cooked, lift out the fish and potato using a spider and leave to cool. Keep the milk for the sauce.

Make a stiff sauce with the flour and butter, add the egg and then add the strained, reserved milk. Combine with the fish and potatoes and finish by adding the chopped chives and parsley and a squeeze of lemon juice. Place in the fridge to chill and set.

Portion in silicone moulds. *Pane* and eat!

A FAVOURITE POEM

I wrote this out for my father when he was ill, and he loved it. I would take my sons' drawings (the boys were then aged five and four) to him in hospital. He would hold them and say 'How lovely darling, now put them in the bin,' which always made me laugh and still does now as I think about it.

I thank thee God, that I have lived
In this great world and known its many joys:
The songs of birds, the strongest sweet scent of hay,
And cooling breezes in the secret dusk;
The flaming sunsets at the close of day,
Hills and the lovely, heather-covered moors;
Music at night, and the moonlight on the sea,
The beat of waves upon the rocky shore
And wild white spray, flung high in ecstasy;
The faithful eyes of dogs, and treasured books,
The love of Kin and fellowship of friends
And all that makes life dear and beautiful.

I thank Thee too, that there has come to me
A little sorrow and sometimes defeat,
A little heartache and the loneliness
That comes with parting and the words 'Good-bye';
Dawn breaking after weary hours of pain,
When I discovered that night's gloom must yield
And morning light break through to me again.

Because of these and other blessings poured
Unasked upon my wondering head,
Because I know that there is yet to come
An even richer and more glorious life,
And most of all, because Thine only Son
Once sacrificed life's loveliness for me,
I thank Thee, God, that I have lived.

Elizabeth Craven

III

Meat

Respecting the ingredients we use is vital. Coming from Scotland we grew up understanding what was involved in a deer stalk: waking early, walking for miles through bogs and mud, shooting the animal and cooking it yourself. There is something special about that. Treating meat simply so that you can appreciate all the interesting flavours is also so important. Thinking about what to have with the meat means paying attention to what is in season, and then things just end up tending to work.

I like to eat meat not too often, actually, which means that it is special when I do.

MINT AND LAMB MEATBALLS

500g organic lamb mince
1 onion
1 clove of garlic
Mixed herbs
3 courgettes
Mint

Take the mince and add a finely chopped onion, pressed garlic and either some dried mixed herbs or fresh finely chopped herbs (parsley, thyme, rosemary). Combine into little balls, which you can then gently fry in some oil. At the same time, fry the courgettes (I cut these into half rounds and then quarters) around the meatballs. Scatter the mint on top for the last minute of cooking. The mint elevates the meatballs and goes so well with the courgettes.

We love these with new potatoes.

DF SF GF WF
Full of vitamin C thanks to the courgettes.

BEST BURGERS

You can't beat these simple burgers that my mother has always made. Just four ingredients ... I am not a fan of adding an egg to bind or breadcrumbs to the mince – it's not needed. These hold together perfectly without.

500g of very good organic lean beef mince
2 onions
A big bunch of parsley
1 clove of garlic, pressed
A slice of smoked streaky bacon per burger
A generous slice of cheddar per burger

Put the onions in a magimix and pulse for a second or two. Place the meat on top, and the parsley and garlic on top of that. Pulse gently until the ingredients are just combined, but be careful not to over-mix, otherwise the mixture will look pale and very unattractive. You are looking for a lightly mixed, parsley-rich meat mixture.

Season the burgers and cook in a frying pan (whilst the bacon is grilling) for a couple of minutes on each side. Place in a buttered bap with the bacon and cheese on top.

41

LAMB CHOPS WITH SALSA VERDE

We have a lean mean grilling machine which someone gave us as a wedding present. I groaned in a spoilt way when it arrived, as I hate clutter building up in the house and it is quite large. However, I now use this so often that every time I turn it on I say a silent thank-you to our genrous friend. Griddling chops is one of its many useful merits.

Salsa Verde is the best sauce in the world for meat, I think, and I would encourage you to make and eat it at all times, with all meat: steaks, chops, everything in fact.

Salsa Verde
2 bunches of parsley
1 bunch of basil
1 bunch of mint
A handful of cornichons, roughly chopped
A handful of capers, roughly chopped
3 anchovy fillets, finely chopped
1 clove of garlic, pressed
1 tablespoon of Dijon mustard
3 tablespoons of red wine vinegar
8 tablespoons of olive oil

Chop up all the herbs and place in a bowl. Add the chopped cornichons and capers. Add the anchovies, the garlic, the Dijon and the vinegar. Slowly add the oil, stirring to create a fragrant masterpiece. Pour it over your cooked chops.

DF GF WF

ZANDER'S MEATBALLS

My cousin, Alexander Montgomerie, is now a hugely popular DJ, touring the globe as Zander. He enjoys eating these at his student digs, and his desperately uncool cousin and her children enjoy them too.

Organic beef meatballs
1 white onion
A tin of tomatoes
Mozzarella cheese, grated
Fresh pasta

Grill the meatballs for 4 minutes until cooked through. Meanwhile, fry the onion in a little butter, and add the tomatoes and simmer. Place the meatballs and sauce in a dish, sprinkle the cheese on top and place under the grill. Cook the fresh pasta and serve with a green salad.

LIL'S CHICKEN CURRY

Perhaps don't rely on this recipe to be ready exactly within the 10-minute promise. I think 15 minutes is possibly more accurate, but it is just too good to leave out.

The great thing about this is that it's all in one pan, so the washing-up is quick too.

Olive oil
Half a chopped onion
A handful of chopped parsley
Third of a teaspoon of mild curry powder
1 tablespoon of tomato paste
1 tablespoon of mango chutney
A tablespoon of chopped dried apricots (if you don't have them raisins work well too)
1 chicken breast, cut into strips
Spinach
2 carrots, chopped into little pieces
Peas
Chopped sweet potato
2 or 3 tablespoons of plain yoghurt
Chicken stock
Rice

Put the rice on to boil with about half a cup of chicken stock, or if you are using stock cubes put half a cube in the water.

In your pan put a bit of olive oil, add the onions,

sweet potato and the carrots let them fry for about 3 minutes, add the chicken for another 4 minutes to brown slightly.

Add the curry powder and the tomato paste, apricots / raisins and mango chutney, then stir so the chicken and carrot and sweet potato are covered in the paste. Add the stock (you will decide now how liquidy you want your curry, I add just enough so that the vegetables and chicken can simmer and cook through in it but not so that it's like soup). Let simmer for 4 minutes, add the spinach and peas and cook for a further 2 mins. Add the parsley.

Your rice should be cooked by now so remove from heat and sieve.

Let your curry cool down a bit and when it has cooled enough add the yoghurt, stir well and serve to your little piglets.

As Lil says: 'Suitable for infants, as I blended this and gave it to Lucas when he was 7 months old (he had been eating since he was 4 months – but don't want to piss any ragey mothers off!)'

GF WF
Full of vitamin A thanks to the sweet potato and iron from the apricots.

Steak and a Perfect Sauce

*As my sons grow older and taller, they are beginning
to crave steaks. I too remember that urge while I was
growing, like a giraffe, to nearly six foot. It would always
be a last-night-of-the-holidays treat steak, and that is
now what I do for the boys.*

*This sauce is unbeatable and a dreamy accompaniment
to the meat.*

For the sauce
  15g unsalted butter
  2 small shallots, finely chopped
  3 sprigs of thyme, leaves picked
  Salt and lots of pepper
  2 teaspoons of Dijon mustard
  1 teaspoon of grainy mustard
  100ml red wine
  100g crème fraiche

Melt the butter, adding the shallots, thyme and
seasoning and cook for a few minutes until the shallots
are soft. Stir in the mustards and then deglaze the pan
with the wine and reduce for a couple of minutes.
Stir in the crème fraiche and check the seasoning.

GF WF

CHILLI CHICKEN

This recipe was given to me by a wonderful photographer who was mad about chillies. We exchanged recipes, and this has been so popular ever since. I usually marinade the chicken pieces in the sauce overnight, but obviously the 10-minute rule in this book meant that I have changed the recipe a little, but when you have more time do try the sauce recipe as a marinade for exceptional results.

4 chicken breasts

For the sauce
1 tablespoon of sunflower oil
2 tablespoons of sesame oil
1 tablespoon of Dijon mustard
2 tablespoons of soy sauce
1 tablespoon of rice vinegar
1 teaspoon of chilli flakes
3 spring onions
1 chilli
A bunch of basil, chopped

Cut the chicken breasts into strips, and heat up a little pan. Gently fry the chicken pieces in a little oil for a few minutes. Combine all of the sauce ingredients and whisk them together. Pour this sauce into the pan with the chicken, warm through and raise the heat until it is simmering. Remove from the heat and enjoy with some grains or pulses, like rice, lentils or quinoa, and a lovely salad to balance it all perfectly.

DF

'There is always music amongst the trees in the garden
but our hearts must be very still to hear it'

IV

Pasta

I grew up with a nanny for eight years who was and remains part of the family. When she comes to visit us now, every time without fail I ask her if she can cook us macaroni cheese. That might well be my desert island choice. Creamy, full of mature cheddar, unfailingly satisfying, absolute heaven. Actually, I haven't included macaroni cheese in this section but pasta at the right time is completely delicious, like all Italian food. You can of course use rice pasta or gluten-free variants for all of the following recipes.

Savannah's Orzo

'Here is my recipe, slightly stolen and adapted from Nigella, that kids and adults will love.'

Bacon
Frozen peas
Orzo (tiny rice-shaped pasta)
Parmesan

Chop the bacon into tiny bits; you can use pre-cubed pancetta if it's easier, but my children prefer smoked back bacon.

Gently fry the bacon until it is starting to brown and the fatty bits are cooking.

Add the frozen peas and stir around the pan until they no longer look frosty.

Add the orzo (I use about a handful per person).

Stir it around for about 30 seconds until it is coated with bacon juices, then pour boiling water over it (two parts water to one part orzo, so if you use a mug to measure out your orzo chuck two mugs of boiling water over it).

Leave simmering for about 10 minutes until it is cooked through. Add more water if it is drying out and your pasta isn't cooked through. The orzo needs to still be in quite a bit of juice for this dish not to dry out, so keep it to the consistency of risotto.

Add a generous handful of finely grated Parmesan and stir in with the pan off the heat.

TORTIE'S WATERCRESS PESTO LINGUINE

When I moved out of London in 2009 I landed, much to my complete luck and joy, next door to Tortie and her husband JF. They could not have been kinder to me in my first few days in the country. Tortie would appear with biscuits for the removal men, and delicious food from their fridge as a present when they were going away. Now that we have come back to the same village, they sadly have moved, but I will always remember those days and all the people who made the transition so much easier than it could have been.

1 packet of fresh watercress leaves
1 lemon, the juice and zest
Handful of pine nuts
1 clove of garlic
Hunk of Parmesan cheese, grated
Swig of good quality olive oil
Packet of dried linguine
Pancetta bits

Whizz up all the above ingredients (except the linguine and pancetta) in a mini processor – add more olive oil if required.

Cook linguine so that it is al dente.

Drain the pasta and mix in the pesto mix immediately. Serve in warm bowls with more Parmesan and / or some fried pancetta bits on top.

Full of vitamin A and calcium from the watercress.

Emma's Basil Pesto

Emma, like Tortie, was a neighbour in the village that I moved to in 2009. I had never met Emma before, yet she appeared in my first few days with her daughter, carrying a cake which had written in icing 'WELCOME TO CHARLTON'. It will be this one act that I remember above all else as the most welcoming, beautiful gesture of kindness. When we moved back to the village in 2014, Emma appeared again with another cake saying 'WELCOME BACK TO CHARLTON'. A very special lady.

175ml extra virgin olive oil
3 roughly chopped garlic cloves
75g of fresh basil
50g of pine nuts
50g of Parmesan, grated

'Put the extra virgin olive oil and garlic cloves into a food processor and whizz briefly. Add the basil and whizz briefly again. Scrape sides down and add the pine nuts. Whizz again and lastly add the Parmesan. Season, and add more oil if necessary. One final whizz but don't overdo it.

'Put the pesto into lots of small containers and then freeze. It freezes beautifully and defrosts very quickly.

'I add the pesto to spaghetti or pasta and that is delicious in itself. Or you could add leftover chicken to the pasta and pesto and add a bit of crème fraiche. I also put the pesto under the skin of a chicken fillet or thighs and pop that in the oven for 20 minutes, or a couple of teaspoons under the skin of a whole chicken before roasting. My children love it on a piece of salmon fillet topped with sliced cherry tomatoes and mozzarella, which I then bake for 15 minutes. You can drizzle it over lamp chops once they are cooked – the possibilities are endless.'

V SF GF WF
Full of vitamin A and C thanks to the basil.

MY FAVOURITE TUNA PASTA

I adore this recipe and it takes seconds to make.

Pasta
1 jar of very good quality tuna in olive oil
1 large bunch of flat-leaf parsley
1 garlic clove
1 red chilli
A very generous scrunching of pepper and some salt

Put your chosen pasta in a large, salted pan of boiling water.

Place the tuna in the magimix, along with all of the other ingredients. Whizz up to form a paste and slowly add some of the oil from the tuna jar until you have a smooth sauce. Once you have drained the pasta (keeping back a small cup of the cooking water), add the sauce to the pasta, stirring and adding some of that cooking water to the pasta until you have achieved loose, coated pasta. Heaven.

Full of vitamin A, B6 and B12 thanks to the tuna.

JULIET'S CHICKEN AND
SUN-DRIED TOMATO PASTA

Pasta
1 small onion
3 chicken breasts
Large handful of sun-dried tomatoes
100ml double cream
Large handful of basil

'Chop the onion and fry in a little butter. Chop the chicken breast into small pieces and add to pan. Fry for 7 minutes and make sure chicken pieces are thoroughly cooked. Then add finely chopped sun-dried tomatoes and stir for a minute. Finally, pour over 50ml of double cream. Isabella makes the finishing touches of torn-up basil sprinkled on top!

'Once the children have had their share of their favourite pasta, I put salt, pepper and some dried chilies for Max and me to tuck into! I hope that you enjoy it as much as we do.'

CHARLOTTE'S COURGETTE PASTA

Charlotte is a spectacularly talented painter, specialising in prints for children and paintings. All four of mine have her 'Dear God, Bless …' prints above their beds.

'My children are pretty good on veg, they've never been given any choice in the matter, so they love this but I appreciate this might be a hard sell with many…'

Grate 1 or 2 courgettes on thick grater.

Penne into salted boiling water.

Grate plenty of Parmesan.

About 6 minutes before penne is ready, heat tablespoon of olive oil in saucepan and fry grated courgette on a lowish heat until softened but still bright green (NOT sludgy green).

Add tablespoon of rinsed capers (capers in salt are much nicer than those in brine).

Serve pasta with a dollop of courgette on top, followed by squeeze of fresh lemon juice, a grating of pepper and plenty of Parmesan.

Full of vitamin C thanks to the courgettes.

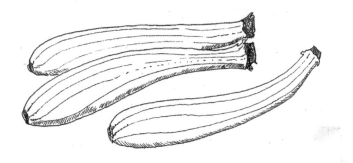

'Nothing improves scenery like ham and eggs'
Mark Twain

V

Eggs

*M*uch as I would love to embrace the good life fully, there are limits imposed by other factors. Our thoughtful bull terrier couldn't resist savaging our guinea pigs and would undoubtedly have eaten pet chickens, so we haven't got round to introducing these yet. In the meantime, I thank Mabel Brown whose brown eggs taste absolutely wonderful and make everything sing with their fluoro-orange yolks. Otherwise we are spoilt for choice with local wonderful eggs, as I am sure are you.

It is the simple things in life that give so much pleasure, and as I said in the introduction I have included the boiled and scrambled egg recipes – not to be ridiculous but just as memory joggers.

Eggs are a good source of vitamin D, the sunshine vitamin, which in Britain, let's face it, is sometimes in short supply.

Asparagus with Mushrooms and a Poached Egg

This is a delicious pile of wonder. English asparagus, one of the few things that remains truly seasonal with its short picking time, is always such a treat.

Enough asparagus for everyone
A large Portobello mushroom per person
2 cloves of garlic, sliced finely
An egg per person
120g unsalted butter
A couple of sprigs of thyme

Chop off the woody ends of the asparagus and steam for 3 minutes until firm but cooked. Put your eggs on to poach in a pan of salted water. Melt the butter in a pan on a medium heat, add the sliced mushrooms, the garlic and a few sprigs of thyme. Gently fry for a few minutes, season, and once golden remove from the pan. Place the asparagus on the plates, followed by the mushrooms and topped with the poached egg. Grind some pepper over the top, and enjoy the wonderful colours on your plate.

V SF GF WF

Tash's Eggy Bread

'At the heart of every 10-minute solution I have for the children are eggs, cucumber and tomatoes. A Sunday-night-tea favourite when I have nothing left to give is eggy bread with chopped-up cucumber and tomatoes on the side.'

Break 2 eggs into a bowl and stir with a fork.

Soak the bread in egg on both sides (about a minute on each side).

Melt some butter in a frying pan.

Fry the bread for about 2 minutes on each side and serve.

Chop up some tomatoes and cucumber and serve with the eggy bread so that you feel some vague nutrients are getting in too!

V

BEN'S EGG IN A CUP

Boil 1–2 eggs per person.

Toast 1 slice of bread per person.

Cut the toast lengthways and then horizontally so that you are left with a pile of small toast squares.

Put the squares into a large bowl, add a generous scoop of butter on top, and a pinch of salt.

Peel the eggs and put them in the bowl. Use a knife and fork to chop up the whole pile of eggs, and stir to make a nice mess.

Serve in large tea cups or small bowls.

Full of vitamin D thanks to the egg.

SPINACH AND CHEDDAR OMELETTE

This was one of my favourite suppers for the boys when they were little. Clearly there are lots of variations on it (use different cheeses like Gruyère, add ham, tomatoes, spring onions, chorizo) but this is our favourite. Serves two children.

3 eggs
A large handful of spinach
A knob of butter
Some grated Dorset cheddar

Melt the butter in a frying pan, whisk the eggs and pour on top of the melted butter. Hold the handful of spinach in your hands and with a pair of scissors chop the bunch into little pieces on top of the eggs. Grate the cheddar all over the pan and season lightly. Cook for about 4 minutes until it looks ready. At this stage I put my frying pan under the grill as I have a detachable handle on our pan, but otherwise you could fold the omelette in half.

V SF GF WF
Full of vitamins A and C and iron thanks to the spinach and vitamin D from the eggs.

SPINACH FRITTERS

250g of courgettes
100g of spinach
A packet of feta
A little mound of grated Parmesan
Half a clove of garlic
Some basil
The zest of 1 lemon
5 organic eggs

Grate the courgettes, shred the spinach and place in a bowl. Crumble in the feta and the Parmesan. Add the finely chopped garlic, the chopped handful of basil and the lemon zest and mix. Season.

Heat some olive oil in a pan, and ladle a tablespoonful of the mixture into the oil, dotting the mixture all over the pan. Flatten into patties and fry for a few minutes and then turn over and repeat.

V SF GF WF
Full of vitamins A and C and iron thanks to the spinach and vitamin C from the courgettes.

SCRAMBLED EGGS

Even with something as simple as scrambled eggs, really good ones take a bit of time and effort.

1 knob of butter
2–3 eggs per person, whisked
Sea salt and fresh pepper
Sourdough

Over a very low heat, melt the butter in a heavy-bottomed pan. Place the eggs in the pan – the eggs must not start to cook as soon as they hit the melted butter. You need to cook them very slowly and gently, always stirring. This will take you about 9 minutes.

Meanwhile toast your sourdough, butter it and then add the eggs.

V
Full of vitamin D thanks to those eggs.

BAKED EGGS

Use one ramekin per child and two per adult.

Eggs
Cream
Cheddar

Put an egg in a ramekin. Pour some cream on top, and decorate with a slice of cheddar and a pinch of salt and grinding of pepper. Place the ramekins in a baking tray and pour boiling water half way up the ramekins, making a bain-marie. Place in a hot oven (200°C) for 9 minutes. Simple and perfect.

V SF GF WF
Full of vitamin D thanks to the eggs.

VI

Bread & Other Delights

'*D*on't forget the marmalade sandwiches' is what *Paddington might say ... but so do I! The humble honey or banana sandwich is a lovely tea if your children have had something more substantial for lunch.*

CROQUE-MONSIEUR

Butter
8 slices of bread
2 tablespoons of plain flour
200ml of milk
160g of Gruyère, grated
Nutmeg
4 tablespoons of Dijon
4 slices of good ham

Turn on your grill and line a tray with foil. Brush one side of each slice of bread with butter and put under the grill butter-side up until toasted. Stir the flour into 50g of melted butter, cook for a minute, then gradually whisk in the milk, a little at a time, until smooth. Simmer for a few minutes, until thickened, then take off the heat and stir in about half of the grated cheese, until it has melted. Grate in a little nutmeg, stir and season lightly.

Spread the untoasted sides of the bread with mustard, put the ham on top, followed by the rest of the cheese, and place under the grill to melt. Once melted, combine the toast slices, with the toasted side uppermost, and push down. Put the sandwiches on to the grill and top with the cheese sauce. Grill for about 5 minutes, until golden and bubbling, and serve immediately.

Jemma's Green Pancakes

This recipe came from our vicar's wife, Jemma. She is the most amazing bread maker and used to sell weekly from her kitchen and various shops locally until they moved. I first met Jemma a few days after we had moved to the country when she drove past me and the boys in my Christiania tricycle. She stopped and wound down her window, and when she found out that we had just moved to the village, she sweetly asked us for Sunday lunch. She then appeared with tomato plants for our garden and showed us such kindness.

Bag of spinach
2 eggs
Organic self-raising flour
Vegetable oil
Milk
Cheddar (optional)

Wilt the spinach in an inch of water in a lidded pan for a few minutes.

Get a frying pan out, put in a bit of butter and set it to heat up.

Squeeze water out of the spinach – just grab it in your hand and squish – doesn't have to be bone dry.

Into the bowl with the spinach, crack 2 eggs. Add 2 heaped tablespoons of self-raising flour and a slug of vegetable oil. Add a couple of tablespoons of milk (not that I ever measure it).

Get your 'soup wand' on your blender and whizz the ingredients together till you get a thick homogenous batter.

Add more milk until you get the right consistency.

Dollop into frying pan and turn over once they've puffed up and set on the first side – maybe 45 seconds each side.

If you feel there's not enough protein in this to call it a proper meal, grate cheese over the pile of pancakes on a plate and flash under the grill.

V SF
Full of vitamins A and C, and iron thanks to the spinach.

CARROT HUMMUS

This is delightfully easy despite the rather long list of ingredients. Well worth the whizz up in the magimix.

2 cups of grated carrot
Half a clove of garlic, peeled
¼ cup of blanched almonds
¼ cup of tahini
¼ cup of extra virgin olive oil
¼ cup of orange juice
1 teaspoon of ground cumin
1 teaspoon of smoked paprika
A handful of coriander

Place all of the above in your magimix, whizz and serve it either on bread or as a dip with yet more carrots, or cucumber sticks.

V DF SF GF WF
Full of vitamin A thanks to the carrots, magnesium from the almonds, vitamin E from the tahini.

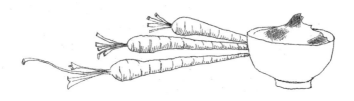

CLASSIC HUMMUS

600g of tinned chickpeas
1 garlic clove
75ml tahini
60ml lemon juice
Parsley
Paprika
Sea salt

Rinse and drain the chickpeas. Add them to a blender with the garlic, tahini, lemon juice and salt. Whizz up and add 6 tablespoons of water. Place in a pretty bowl with a sprinkling of chopped parsley and a sprinkling of paprika all over the hummus. Now drizzle a little extra virgin olive oil on top.

V DF SF GF WF
Full of iron and magnesium thanks to the chickpeas. Vitamin E from the tahini.

GUACAMOLE

Used as a dip, or on toast, you can't go wrong with this fresh and delicious bowlful of goodness.

1 green chilli
Juice of 2 limes
3 avocados
Big bunch of coriander

Finely chop the chilli and add to the lime juice and mashed avocadoes. Combine with the chopped coriander, season carefully and place in a lovely bowl.

V DF SF GF WF
Rich in potassium, fibre and antioxidants, the avocado is a powerhouse of goodness.

CHEESE ON TOAST

Unbelievably obvious but still a Sunday night joy for us. We razzle ours up a bit with some chopped spring onions, a green chilli and coriander but you may prefer to have yours like the boys do, just with Lea and Perrins. Still a perfect, simple supper.

COURGETTES, MINT AND FETA

This really is one of the best recipes in the book. I could eat this every day and never get bored – so fresh, so delicious, so good. Served with some sourdough, I think you really can't get better. I've lost count of the times I have written this recipe out for friends.

Courgettes, sliced lengthways into ribbons, as thin as you can
Bunch of mint, chopped
Packet of good feta
A shallot

For the dressing
6 tablespoons of olive oil
2 tablespoons of white wine vinegar
Half a teaspoon of sugar
Good pinch of salt
Good amount of pepper

Griddle the courgettes, having wiped them with a little olive oil once sliced. You want those wonderful char marks all down them. Then lay them on a beautiful big dish. Finely chop the shallot and scatter over the courgette. Crumble the feta all over, and then chop the mint all over that. Drizzle the dressing over the top. Heaven.

Full of vitamin A, potassium and antioxidants thanks to the courgettes and mint.

VII

Rice

*I*adore rice, instantly satisfying and coming in so many different varieties. I love them all. My favourite method is probably to mix them up: wild, basmati and red, but whatever your preference is – brown, white or pilau from the Indian takeaway – it is all wonderful.

Tomatoes and Rice

This little dish is one that my Father used to make so it always makes me happy thinking of him. It is so simple, so comforting and so delicious.

Enough organic basmati rice for each person
2 tins of chopped tomatoes
2 onions
Organic cheddar

Put the rice on to cook, and start chopping the onions into fine dice. Gently fry in a bit of butter and oil, and then add the tomatoes. Once the rice is ready, add to the tomato sauce with a very generous mound of grated cheese. Stir and combine all the ingredients, season and serve with a little green salad.

V SF GF WF
Full of vitamin C and A thanks to the tomatoes.

Fried Rice

I remember eating this for the first time as a child and loving it. I had never tried soy sauce before and found it to be extremely exotic and exciting.

Basmati rice
Peas
Bacon or pancetta
Bunch of spring onions
1 medium leek, halved and washed
Tamari soy sauce
Sesame oil
2 eggs

Cook your rice and at the same time grill some bacon, 2 rashers per person. Put your peas on to boil (a bowl full), chop up the spring onions and the leek, and gently fry for a couple of minutes. Heat some sesame oil in a different pan and add the eggs, stir with a wooden spoon to break them up and scramble them. Add the drained rice, the chopped-up bacon, peas and spring onions and leeks. Sprinkle the soy sauce over the rice for the final stir and add more to taste for the grown-ups.

DF SF GF WF
Full of vitamin C thanks to the spring onions, vitamin A from the leeks, and vitamin C from the peas.

INDIAN RICE

350g of your favourite rice
200g of sliced mushrooms
1 onion, finely chopped
1 clove of crushed garlic
1 red pepper, chopped and de-seeded
125g of green beans, chopped
1 tablespoon of curry powder
1 teaspoon of cumin seeds
A bowl full of peas
Handful of coriander, chopped

Cook the rice until it is tender, usually 10 minutes. At the same time, heat up some oil and fry the mushrooms, onion, garlic, pepper and green beans for a few minutes until softened. Add the curry powder and cumin and peas, cooking for another couple of minutes. By this time the rice should be ready; drain and add to the pan. Once you have seasoned the rice, sprinkle it with coriander and serve.

V DF SF GF WF
Full of vitamin A thanks to the pepper, vitamin B from the mushrooms, calcium from the green beans.

RICE SALAD

I can't remember where this recipe appeared from, but it really is a cupboard back-up for us, and great in the summer especially. It is important to use very good tuna that you find in delis or some good supermarkets.

A jar of tuna in oil
Good olives
Tin of organic sweetcorn
Tomatoes, chopped
Rice
Parsley, chopped

Cook your rice and add to all of the remaining ingredients. Season and eat with a green salad.

DF SF GF WF
Full of vitamins B12 and A thanks to the tuna, vitamin C from the tomatoes and vitamins A and C from the parsley.

VIII

Puddings

*L*orcan and Bertie are always saying 'Mum, what's for pudding except for yoghurt or fruit?' When I reply, inevitably, yoghurt or fruit, they say 'Oh Mummmmm, today we had waffles at school with chocolate sauce' or something else that they found equally as exciting. They are absolutely mad about puddings and I don't make enough of them. I do make a lot of cakes, but sadly none can be made within the 10-minute time slot, hence they are not listed here.

I hope you enjoy what is included.

Bridget's Coconut Milk Pudding

'This can cook while the children are eating their main course.'

4–5 tablespoons of ground rice
1 litre carton of coconut milk
1 tablespoon of coconut oil

Spoon ground rice into a pudding basin.
 Pour on milk and stir.
 Dot coconut oil on the top.
 Bake in oven at 200°C for 10 minutes.
 Serve with a spoonful of jam or honey.

V DF GF WF
Full of lauric acid thanks to the coconut milk which can kill bacteria and viruses.

APPLE SNOW

500g of cooking apples
2 tablespoons of lemon juice
50g of caster sugar
2 egg whites

Peel, core and slice the apples and put in a saucepan with the lemon juice and sugar. Cover and cook over a low heat until the apples are very soft and then blend with a stick blender. Spread out on a china plate and pop outside to cool quickly whilst you whisk up the egg whites. Fold them into the apple purée and serve in a glass.

V GF WF
High in fibre and vitamin C thanks to the apples.

Mango Hedgehog

The very charming and delightfully simple pudding of a little mango hedgehog is as easy as this.

Cut through the mango as close to the central stone as possible, slicing off a big chunk either side of it. Next, take the pieces that you have cut away and score horizontal and vertical lines in the flesh, making a grid, being careful not to pierce the skin. Push the flesh up through, bending the edges out, to reveal an upturned spiky hedgehog.

V DF SF GFWF
High in vitamin C and A.

Raw Banana Flapjack

This is so utterly delicious and quick and easy, and enjoyed by all. I make a lot of raw treats like these, adding whatever is to hand. Sometimes I chuck in a handful of dried cranberries, raisins or dried un-sulphured apricots. You can have fun adjusting to suit yourself.

350g of organic porridge oats
A good squeeze of honey
6 medjool dates, finely chopped
3 bananas whizzed up in a magimix to a purée

Combine all the ingredients in a large bowl and push it into a lined square tin.

Pop this in the fridge to set for a while. It will keep for five days in the fridge but is bound to be eaten much before.

V DF SF GF* WF
A good source of vitamin C and potassium, thanks to the bananas.
* Provided gluten-free oats are used.

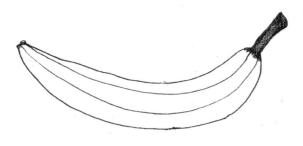

LAURA'S BANANAS AND YOGHURT

The chopped banana and yoghurt pudding is one that never grows old and is churned out endlessly for my children. I tend to use goats' or sheep's yoghurt, which I much prefer to dairy yoghurt. I then squeeze some agave nectar on top, and chuck on any berries that are to hand.

'Here's my recipe. A pudding, which seeing as mine barely eat a scrap, is a winner.'

Banana
Yoghurt
Vanilla extract
Granola
Hundreds and thousands

Chop one banana and put in the bottom of a ramekin or small bowl. Fill with poring yog, vanilla and top with crunchy granola (Lizi's is the best) and sprinkle with hundreds and thousands...

'5 mins, tops!'

A good source of vitamin C and potassium thanks to the banana.

Serious Smoothie for Exhausted Parents and Children

This is so delicious and has saved me several times when I have had a late night and perhaps an early start. It lifts the spirits and we all adore it at breakfast time. The avocado makes it very creamy and the lemon makes it sing.

Three-quarters of an avocado
Half a lemon
500ml apple juice
An inch of ginger, cut very finely

Blend all the ingredients for a minute until you are sure it is smooth and pour.

V DF SF GF WF
Full of fibre, vitamins K, A and C thanks to the avocado, with anti-inflammatory properties thanks to the ginger and more vitamin C thanks to the lemon. An all-round super drink.

Emily's Smoothie

1 banana
1 kiwi
A few spoons of yoghurt
1 sachet of probiotic powder
Pomegranate seeds

Blitz the first four ingredients in a blender and sprinkle with pomegranate seeds.

V SF GF WF
Full of vitamin C thanks to the kiwi.

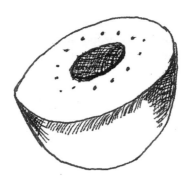

Marina's Brazilian Bananas

Marina is the genius, with her husband Phil, behind the children's clothing label Waddler. She lives in a house they built on an island off Brazil, with her three boys, living a dream.

2 bananas for each hungry person
Butter
Cinnamon
Sugar

Peel bananas and cut them lengthways. In a frying pan add 1 tablespoon of butter and fry the bananas first on one side, then the other, until they are deliciously golden brown. Then pop on a plate and sprinkle cinnamon and sugar over them and eat immediately.

V GF WF
A good source of potassium and vitamin C, thanks to the banana.

DAWNY'S MANGO AND YOGHURT

Dawny has been a big part of our lives since meeting her when Pom Pom was born in 2012. She comes each week to have tea with us, and we all adore her. Being seventy-nine doesn't stop her in any respect, the babies insist on being chased down the corridor and Dawny hurls herself onto the beanbag to squeals of laughter.

  1 ripe mango, peeled
  Quarter of a big pot of Greek yoghurt
  2 drops of vanilla essence
  1 ripe passion fruit, seeds scooped out

Mash the flesh of the mango and combine with the other ingredients.

SF GF WF
A good source of vitamins C and A, thanks to the mango.

BANANA SPLIT

4 bananas
8 scoops of ice cream (I use vanilla)
Some hazelnuts
Dark chocolate
50g of butter
A tablespoon of golden syrup

Put a packet of chocolate, broken up, in a bowl above a simmering pan of water and melt with the butter and the syrup.

Turn on the oven (about 180°C) and place a handful of hazelnuts in a mug. Use a rolling pin to smash down into the hazelnuts, always fun for the children, and then put the nuts scattered over a baking tray into the oven to toast for 5 minutes, bringing out all their flavours.

Meanwhile, peel the bananas and cut lengthways, placing on either side of each plate. Put a scoop full of ice cream in between, drizzle the chocolate sauce over the bananas and sprinkle some of the hazelnuts over the top.

GF WF
A good source of potassium and vitamin C thanks to the banana.

Scotch Pancakes

I was brought up on these pancakes made by our much adored nanny, Dian. Like Little Black Sambo, I could eat one hundred and sixty-nine of these treats. Very quick, and oh so delicious.

100g of self-raising flour
2 tablespoons of caster sugar
1 egg
50g of melted butter
120ml of milk

Mix the flour and sugar together. Make a well in the middle and put in the beaten egg and melted butter and milk to make it the consistency of thick cream. Do not beat though; combine it lightly. Drop spoonfuls of the mixture onto a hot, greased frying pan and cook for about 2–3 minutes until bubbles rise to the surface and burst. Turn the pancakes over and cook until the underside is golden. Place the cooked pancakes between a folded-over dishcloth on a wire rack. Serve with butter and jam.

V

GEORGIE'S MILKSHAKE

Georgie is the co-founder of Dotty Dungarees, the perfect replacement for the old Oshkosh.

I always feel like a milkshake is such a treat and this one is also surprisingly healthy. Amazing for the exhausting months after you've had a baby, when it feels like you never will sleep a straight night ever again and need a good breakfast to make it through the day, or for a healthy snack for a toddler on the move or indeed as a pudding.

Here are some ingredients you could use (alter everything to taste!) which just need to be thrown in a blender.

Half a pint of milk
1 banana
1 teaspoon of honey
4 tablespoons of cereal
2 ice cubes
And endless extras if you want, e.g. strawberries, blueberries, vanilla, peanut butter etc.

PINK FIZZY DELIGHT

Perhaps one of the healthiest fizzy drinks that you could give a child, it is absolutely delicious and looks so exciting in a jug. The colour is pink and glorious, and you can happily keep on pouring knowing that every glass is doing wonders.

Half a small raw beetroot
1 apple
Quarter of a pineapple
Half of an unwaxed lemon (with rind on)
1 litre of sparkling water

Juice the beetroot, the apple, the pineapple and the lemon. Add to the sparkling water in a jug. Joy.

V DF SF GF WF
Full of vitamin C thanks to the pineapple and lemon. High in fibre thanks to the apple. The beetroot helps to build blood, make white blood cells and increase antioxidants. It is one of the most important vegetables for our health.

JOOLS' CHOCOLATE AND
BANANA TOASTIES

Jools is an incredible cook and lives with her husband …
and pet tarantula Molly.
This is the kind of pudding that I adore but don't eat
too often on health grounds.

Chocolate loaf
Nutella
Banana

'You need 2 slices of chocolate loaf per person (found in enormous supermarkets). Remove the crusts from the bread and butter one side of each slice thinly. Spread the unbuttered side with either Cadbury's chocolate spread or Nutella.

'Get a non-stick frying pan and place one slice of bread in it, buttered side down. Slice a banana onto the upturned chocolate spread side, in the pan, making it as flat as possible, and then slap the other piece of bread, butter side up, onto the banana.

'Fry over a medium heat until the bread has browned slightly (not exactly easy, as the bread is brown anyway!) and gone crispy. Flip the sandwich over with a fish slice to crisp the other side, pressing the whole down to stick it all together.

Cut into quarters, diagonally to serve, with cream or ice cream. Devour any leftovers quickly, before anyone sees!

'I find that making them by this method, in a frying pan, is so much easier than struggling with a toasted sandwich maker, which is so difficult to clean.'

RHUBARB COMPOTE

Beautiful pink stems of rhubarb are such an excitement. So easy: chop into little chunks, put in a pan with a very small amount of water and gently stew down within about 5 minutes. Serve with a blob of your favourite yoghurt and a squeeze of honey if you would like to sweeten it.

This of course can be done with apples: simply peel, core and chop into pieces and repeat as for the rhubarb compote.

V GF WF
A good source of magnesium thanks to the rhubarb.

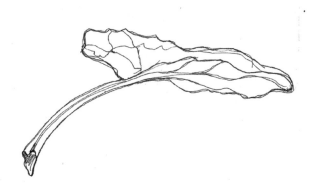

MIA'S GENIUS ICE CREAM

Purchase your favourite yoghurt tubes and place them in the freezer. You can then serve them as healthy ice creams which the kids can suck on.

Preparation time – 5 seconds.

MIRANDA'S BEDTIME RECIPE
FOR SOUND SLEEP

Dormir con los Angeles

'Gentle Jesus meek and mild look upon this little child.'

And then together we say: 'God bless ... x y and z' (i.e. the family, friends and pets. In Benj's case sometimes chicken and chips are also asked to be blessed!)

'I see the moon and the moon sees me...

God bless the moon, and God bless me.

Star light, star bright,

The first star I see tonight.

I wish I may, I wish I might, have the wish I wish tonight.'

A Clutch of Blank Pages for Your Own Notes

POPPY'S DIRECTORY

Listed below are people and places that are mostly local to me, and which I wanted to share. They are exceptional in their individual ways, and should you find yourselves by the borders of Dorset and Wiltshire, I highly recommend a visit. They are not only friends but come with 5 gold-star endorsements. I could not rate them more highly.

• The Ludwell Village Stores – I mentioned Jo and Phil in the introduction. This shop has won the Champion of Champions award, which means that it was voted the best village shop in Great Britain, for very good reason. It is a tiny shop of incredible, high quality, locally produced goods. It is faultless in every respect. It also has a coffee machine behind the counter producing the best coffee I have ever had.

• Pyt House – this is an old walled garden, which is now a restaurant / café with a deli counter. It is the most dreamy setting you could imagine for a restaurant, nestled amongst an incredible working garden. I go each week delivering my chocolate biscuit cake, and love watching the garden change throughout the seasons.

• The Beckford Arms – this is a delicious, very comfortable pub set on the Fonthill Estate. I am not very keen on hotels, but I did spend a night here on my birthday a few years ago, and I think it was as close as you can get to a perfect stay.
T: 01747 870385.

• Jenny Hummel – an extremely successful remedial masseuse, who is as good as you can ever hope to imagine. She regularly treats Olympians and lesser beings such as me.
T: 07958 663267

• Georgina Rhodes – an extraordinary five-element Chinese herbalist and acupuncturist. I don't say this lightly, but Georgina works miracles. She takes twelve different pulses from your wrists and will be able to tell you exactly what is going on in your body. I would travel huge distances to be treated by Georgina.
T: 01935 422488

• Ros Nelmes – Ros is a McTimoney chiropractor and, like Georgina, she can tell what is going on in your body, but this time with your bones, and gently manipulates them back into place. No scrunching, just very subtle taps. Ros shines out like a beacon of white light amid the rather strange environment of Blandford.
T: 01258 860793

• Libbie Cordle – physiotherapist. Libbie has an enormous following locally and is a specialist in neuro-musculoskeletal work.
T: 0870 220 2267

• The Toy Box, Shaftesbury – a very old-fashioned, very well-stocked stationers and toy shop. I spend hours looking at their selection of pens and sheets of card, the Playmobil selection and the pencils. It is how toy shops should be, and the smell is so reminiscent of my childhood spent in the Inverness bookshop Melvins.

• Clementine's, Lower Lawn Barns, Fonthill Gifford – set amongst a courtyard with bantams and chickens freely clucking around, this is a hidden gem of a shop. Beautifully stocked with gifts for all ages, it is impossible to come out of here empty-handed. It was the first shop to stock Mrs Todd's Candles: unmistakable, beautiful hand-poured candles that I can't resist buying.

• Kensons Farm, Sutton Mandeville – I mentioned Liz and Hugh in the introduction and I thank my lucky stars that we live near them. I once went on one of their organic vegetable-growing courses. Very much the novice amongst gurus, it didn't take me long to think that actually continuing to buy all Kensons' vegetables from the market, once a week, was perhaps the way forward.* Who knows, maybe I will get there growing my own, but until then I am so happy turning up at this shed, and filling the honesty box once my arms are full. There are twenty-six acres here, full of goodness and extremely happy produce. The shed is open twice a week but just ring the bell if you arrive on another day and someone will appear to help.

• Quentin Shaw – osteopath in Tunbridge Wells. I say this with all seriousness, not Quentin's claim, but mine – this man has X-ray vision. He sees what is going on with your skeleton. I had a problem whilst I was expecting, of severe SPD, which left me in a wheelchair for most of my pregnancies. I discovered Quentin during my fourth pregnancy and he kept me mobile. I would travel on a five-hour round trip just to see Quentin for twenty minutes, worth every moment. He is a genius. Any back problems, I cannot recommend him more.

• Danuta Mazur – a facialist whom I was fortunate enough to discover when I was twenty. Danuta was trained up by Eve Lom and she has her own practice off High Street Kensington in London. Danuta is an angel with healing gifts and you come away with glowing skin and a restored soul having seen her.
T: 0203 011 0355

• Beauly, near Inverness – I grew up in the Highlands and this is really where my heart is. Going home to Scotland does something to my soul and although I couldn't be happier in Dorset, for me the balance of being down south for term time and in Scotland for the holidays is perfect. Beauly is a treasure-trove of delight: from Campbell's, the finest woollen / tweed shop in Britain, to the deli, to Iain Marr's antiques and Donald the ironmonger, and the best cake shop in Scotland, Harry Gow (get there early otherwise they have sold out) – it's a little one-street village with incredibly friendly, charming Scots at every turn.

• Hacienda San Rafael, near Seville – I cannot recommend somewhere more. Tiny, delicious food, family owned, no supper menus, so no decisions to be made, discreet service, peace. Heaven. For a weekend away, I'm not sure what anyone would want that this didn't offer. A hotel, but not as others. A very superior place which just gets it right on every level.
www.haciendadesanrafael.com

• If you should find yourself in Shaftesbury on a Tuesday morning, wondering what to do with your children, head no further than the Arts Centre. Emma's Magic Bag is forty-five minutes of delight, watching Emma enthral all the children and grown-ups. So amazing is Emma that I count these forty-five minutes as weekly therapy for myself. No booking is required.
T: 07983 464202

INDEX

A

almond 73
apple 98, 101
apple
  apple juice 91
  cooking apples 87
artichoke 14
avocado 14, 15, 34, 75, 91

B

bacon 41, 52, 81
banana 69, 89, 90, 92, 93, 95, 97, 99
basmati rice 79, 80, 81
beetroot 98
bread 13, 20, 23, 27, 29, 35, 41, 63, 64, 69, 70, 71, 73, 75, 76,
      99
  sourdough 7, 67, 77
broccoli 7–8
butter beans 15

C

capers 19, 27, 42, 58
carrot 9, 22, 28, 45, 46
caster sugar 87, 96
cereal 97
cheese
  cheddar 41, 51, 65, 68, 71, 80
  feta 7, 14, 66, 77
  Gruyère 65, 70

G

garlic 2, 4, 5, 13, 19, 22, 28, 31, 32, 40, 41, 42, 43, 53, 54, 56, 62, 66, 73, 74, 82
golden syrup 95
granola 90
green beans 82

H

hazelnut 7, 8, 95
honey 33, 69, 86, 89, 97

K

kiwi 92

L

leek 6, 81
lettuce 34
lime 5, 19, 26, 28, 34, 75

M

mango 46, 88, 94
mango chutney 45–6
meat
  bacon 41, 52, 81
  beef 41, 44
    steak 42, 47
  chicken 34, 45–6, 48–9
  ham 25, 60, 65, 70
  lamb 40, 42
  pancetta 52, 53, 81

milk 35–6, 70, 71–2, 96, 97
mint 3, 4, 13, 21, 40, 42, 77

S

samphire 15
spinach 20, 28, 45, 46, 65, 66, 71, 72
spring onions 15, 22, 48–9, 65, 76, 81
sweetcorn 83
sweet potato 45–6

T

tahini 73, 74
tomatoes 2, 7–8, 9, 25, 26, 32, 55, 63, 65, 83
  tomato paste 45–6
  sun-dried 14, 15, 57
  tinned 33, 44, 80

Y

yoghurt 45–